Poetry for a Conscious Mind

Afoma Mbara Mpi.

Cover design & Interior Illustrations
by Ben@BenCreatesBooks

Library of Congress Control Number: 2025925982

ISBN: 979-8-9927189-8-0 (hardcover)
ISBN: 979-8-9927189-7-3 (paperback)
ISBN: 979-8-9927189-9-7 (e-book)
ISBN: 979-8-9927189-5-9 (audiobook)

Color Me Clear

You are aware
But for comprehensive examination
Dive Deeper

Some things are novel
Some, it is enough to notice
Some, will need more than an acknowledge

For things that need work
Some, require a tackle
Some, mandate offensive maneuvers
Some, call for a Hail Mary

When it is transformation you seek
All things
Especially those that are dearest
Require a thorough wash and shake
Transparency is vital

Consciousness

To be conscious

Is to have full perspective

A bird's eye view of reality

As it is

To navigate without circumspect

To flow as the moment demands

Without need for respite

No need for speculation

No need to calculate

All alternatives available

In the moment

Moment by moment

SEPARATE SELF

Only the separate self

Worries

Whether or not it is aware

Whether or not it is still present

How present or not it is

How

Whether

Or when

It will disappear

OUTDATED SOFTWARE

Feel the drag

Like the kick start of an old farm engine

It's done hard work

For as long as you've had it

You know it's on its last leg

It probably won't make it full circle back

But habit prevails

You reach for its keys

Your psychological software

Albeit outdated

Keeps running in the background

It hijacks your hardware to do hard labor

Attempting to power and drive

Your computing solutions

It needs an upgrade

Perhaps a complete override

This, you know

But…

HOLLOW
(DEDICATED TO ANTHONY AVIGUETERO)

A Vertical Core

Beyond mind

The space between sounds

Sourced with vitality

Of quiet magnetism

Tis the center for originality

Bursting with ingenuity

The birthplace of melody

Fount of harmony

Spring of life

A Boundless Tapestry

HEAVEN

Between
The earth and its moon
The moon and its shadows
The sun and its rays
The star and its twinkles

Beyond the seas
Across the skies
Within the cloud and its gloom
Under the rain and its wetness

And
From snow to hail
Herein lies Heaven

COMPLICIT RESPONSIBILITY

Caught in a web
Woven with strings
Fine, silky threads of suffering
Carefully woven in ignorance

They are undiscernible
To the unattentive
They ensnare
With the slightest movement
Suffocating
Forcing a continuous return
To the same starting point
Needing lifetimes of effort to detangle

Stay alert!
Wind up the strings
Double up and make a pad
Use it as cushion
Layback

Find, it is home
A Palace
Richness endowed
Worldly pleasures not amiss
Moments of poverty
Of no consequence
Eternal joy abound
Come home to yourself

A Moment

Less than an instant

Never rigid

Non positional

The seedling

The burst of a sapling to life

Each flowering

Already being

But fluid

A cocooned larva

The burst of a butterfly

Away from the cracked cocoon

Continuously becoming

Each a complete moment

Of Cosmic totality

BITTERSWEET

Bitter
Melancholic traces
Around the heart
Memories of endearment
A fondness for time
The past and the imagined

Sweet
Buoyant impulses
From the heart center
Rich as Sugar Plum
Warm as Crimson
Openness of the Heart

THE GOOD ROGUE

She comes with fierce intent
Snatching goodies from clutched hands
Peeling off loose hanging garments
Dispossess of possessions
And
Runs away with a sack of loot
Your most cherished lot
Perhaps all that you own

Bow down in gratitude
For this most despised rogue
May succeed in stripping away
All that is not you
Leaving you bare
Only to face
What you really are

TRAGEDY DEFINED

To incarnate
To live
And
To dissolve
As a human being

Without the experience
Of the magnitude
Of it all

Without knowing
The immensity
How hugely indescribable
Is the "I" in the 'I am'

Without realization
Of the enormity contained
In a piece
Of human life

MY "SELF"

It is a movement

My movement

I call it "self"

Myself

By moving myself

I look different

Appear different

Feel different

From my other movements

In form

"self" assumes identity

And independence

Derived wholly from me

In this form of movement

My attributes are unique

Always reflective as I am
I can't help but move in this manner
I am Persistent
Consistent
Headstrong
With a strong foothold on "self"

And since there is no time
And no distance
Between I and myself
Heaven and earth are mine
To move

Permutations & Combinations

A Grasshopper's bid on earth

A Firefly's summons of fire

A Butterfly's request from wind

A Dragonfly's call to water

A ladybug's double leisure of earth and wind

Permutations and combinations

Invitations of earth and fire

Of wind and water

Uniquely combining aspects of myself

Flowing outwardly in communion

Delighted in my creations

Tiny pieces of me

Multitudes of myself

Expressing flawlessly

A Mistake

As I flex
In my extension
Invariable, perspective is skewed
Sometimes lost
But I snapback
In due course

Do not mistake
A slice of a pie
For the whole
The ray of the sun
For the sun
A moment in eternity
For time

My Brilliant Little Shadow

Inseparable as we are

It wants to be sought

So,

It darts around me

Sometimes before me

Sometimes at my corner

It is brilliant

With hide and seek

Imitative

Unabashed

Looks back at me

Talks back

Holds firm during confrontation

Seeking acknowledgement

Once acknowledged

It no longer has a hold

Its mystery demystified

This dark shadowy side of myself

HEART CENTER

Open and Vast

Expanded to all corners

Out from within

The cosmos arises

Holograms emanate

Mantras reverberate

A voice whispers

Lean in

There's a river of flowing goodness

CHECKS AND BALANCES

Where is input from source directed?

Comfort?

Convenience?

Pleasure?

Avoidance?

Allow the inexplicable magic

Of Source energy

To unfold unto itself

Remarkable Abundant Intelligence

Truth

FLEX AND EXTEND

Where is my operation localized?
In this moment
Where is my center?
Away or at home?
Mind or heart?

I flex to get away
Contracted, in my mind
I see the world and others

I extend to come home
Expanded, in my heart
I see nothing but myself

Upstairs, I flex and reflex
Downstairs, I rest in my abode
As I am

TEXTURES AND WAVES OF SURRENDER

The road to surrender

Is paved with sensations

The entire landscape

Is drawn on the body

Painted with sensational colors

Colors of varying qualities

Waves of unnerving textures

Textures of increasing degrees of amplitude

Unease, Frustration, Sadness

Fear screams the loudest, disguised as Rebellion

All filtered

And Juxtapositioned

Alongside documentary recapitulation

Narrations by the mind

To surrender

Is to clearly hear the screams

To feel the fear

Laydown the palm branches

Let rebellion match on

Viva! la crusade!!

Viva la revolución

When surrender migrates

From thought to being

At the point of recognition

Where thought is not perceived as output

When there is no lapse

Between thought and afterthought

And there is zero distance

Between

The thought of surrender

And

The act of surrender

Surrender happens

Where thinking…sensing…feeling…perceiving

Is happening

As waves of myself

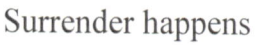

DISCERNMENT

Movement of the mind

Is customary

Through assimilation

It discerns unease in the body

I am aware

Any contradiction is nonconsequential

For unease in the body

And discernment in the mind

Both are movements of myself

NORMALCY

As surrender continuously happens
Body is inclusive of all experience
Its boundaries and outline stretch
Beyond grasp
Physically and psychologically
The surrendered becomes transparent
And
Transposed unto light
As a reflection of myself

When it no longer feels as if
Entire life force is engaged
With the process of surrender
There is plenty of room
For a broader range of phenomenal experience

CALIBRATION

Thinking about surrender

Realizing the necessity of surrender

Surrendering

Recognizing surrender as it happens

Knowing

All are of varying degrees of calibration

Each is revealing

Of a porosity of consciousness

Knowing that surrender ought to happen

And cooperating with surrender

Are not of the same caliber of "self"

Calibration ceases

As the thought of surrender

Is surrendered

As the "self" that is consumed with surrender

Is the very "self" that is consumed and extinguished by
surrender

Do You Know What You Want?

Yesterday was bright from very early

You slept till midday

Waking up off and on

Wishing for rain

Even a glorious vista

And a curtain of morning glories

With vines framing windowpanes

Could not console you

Yester afternoon you spent in a daze

Bewildered

Reminiscing

An image in mind

A promise for tomorrow

Today, the clouds are forming
Yesterday's desires granted
But your expectations vanquished with its grey
Hopes for a picnic amidst fields of sunflowers
Excitement for butterflies enamored with red puppies
Of a happy afternoon
Are no more
Dreams forgone
As a storm slowly brews – inside

What do you really want?
Is it Rain? Thunder? Butterflies?
Red Puppies or Morning Glories?
Or do you just want to be happy?
Yes?

Then why dabble with intermediaries?
The substitutes
The inferior
The inadequate
The insatiable

Why settle for fleeting passion?

Open up to Love

The foundation of my Being

The source of you

Step inside

Come to happiness

Come to Source

EMOTIONS

Resistance

The fear of capitulation

The disdain for concession

The disgust for submission

It separates

The anticipation for resolution

Is attachment

It binds

And why do you chastise your desires?

They are passersby

Spectators with elaborate schemes

They have their own schedule

Acknowledge them

Treat them gently

Pat them on the back

Then set them free on their way

Allow agitation, anxiety, anger

Allow whatever comes

To come and go as it pleases

Let it move freely

Its movement is a mode of transport

From moment to moment

Into infinity

And always in eternity

A Fool's Game

Mind is brilliant
After the fact
Like predicting rain
After seeing thick, dark gray clouds

"The fact" happens
In its absence
While it is preoccupied with stuff
Old news revamped and reconfigured
For use by an insatiable audience
Other brilliant minds

At the junction
The seed point of plantation
Where the flow of creation
Co-joins mind
Mind grabs and usurps
Assembles, disassembles

Configures and deconstructs

In innumerable number of combinations

Memory voluntarily donates distortion

Belief takes care of bias

A fantastically thwarted perspective

Mind's intellectual insight

No matter how coherent its narrative

Pales

In comparison to the Intelligence

That sources the intellect

Consider how much of creation

Actually flows to mind

At the intersection

Where mind impinges on the elements of creation

How much of creation can it hold?

Does what's missing not hint

At the incompleteness

Of phenomenal experience?

FAIR WEATHER FRIEND

On sunny afternoons
On breezy evenings
You wish to hold my hand
To go for a long walk
You hold tight
As if life depends on it

When it rains
You pull away
And seek the nearest shelter
An aluminum roofed trap for lightning
A mosquito infested hole
Anything will suffice
No matter the condition
No matter how ineffective

Why do you only cherish me
When the sun is out?
Is the rain not also my making?
Why tie ropes around me under the sun
And relinquish my allure in the rain?
Why do you run and hide from me
In the thickness of a storm?

Do I not hold my arms out
In the middle of the storm
Ready to embrace you?

Do I gift the rain
With less heart
Than I do the sun?
When it rains
Do I not pour my heart out to you?
Does the rain
Not fall on you
As auspiciously
As does the sun?

And you?
You admonish my first drop
You scold as soon as you feel my touch

Walk in the rain
Allow the rain to wash you clean
Before you dry in the sun
Venture out of the polluted well
Let me pull you out of stagnation
Weather the storm
And set out
To a place infinitely magnetic, unbound

Why do you hesitate?
Vacillate?
Is my love for you not dear?
Do I not come to you upon appeal?
Why do you contract?
Shrink and pull away from my reach
And avoid me
All I desire
Is to reach and pull you closer

Come to me

Hold my hands

Walk with me

Rain or shine

Commit to me

Let us walk through time

Dance through infinity

Unto eternity

PREFERENTIAL TREATMENT

Yesterday, you wanted a Koenigsegg
Today, it's a Polestar you seek
What will it be tomorrow?
See that your preferences are inconstant
Roller coaster of ideas and emotions
Becoming weak, stale or outdated over time
In need of refreshment

Treat your preferences
With keen interest
But lightly and casually
As you would a temporary boarder

ADVENTURE FROM TIME CAPTIVITY

Come
Stay away from time
And step onto a place without landing

Stay with me
Let us journey deep into the abyss
And fall into eternity

Teary Eyes

Wipe away those tears
They blur vision
And distort perspective

Wipe away your tears
See clearly through those eyes
Your visions are of me
Your perceptions are of me

Look at me
Look again!
Eternity is your line of sight
What use are tears?
When you are eternity

My Nemesis

Of course it is I!

Whatever else could possibly have

The overriding

The inescapable

Magnetic pull

Away from me

Except myself?

Who else knows that much about me

Has the inside intel

To engineer my downfall

With such sophisticated logic

And acrobatic maneuvers?

What is gathered of me

Insinuated about me

How much is glimpsed of me

Or perceived of me

Can only be through
Slippage
Rash infliction that is short lived
Stopped abruptly with little given away

Or via intentional leakage
Manufactured, warranted, and distributed
For a specific purpose and effect

Oh, yes!
Whether or not I'm aware in the moment
It matters not
With clarity, I know
My archenemy
Can only be me!

PAIRING ADORATION

Fruits that stain and taint
Seeping through thoroughly
The taste of guava
Seeped into a pear
The color palette of berries
On a napkin
White linen stained yellow
By powder
From a sunflower stigma

Pairing attractions
The vigor of resilient exuberance
Expressions of robust transparency

INDECISION

You've moved away from the curve
The inner edges of the dark line
You journeyed across the striated band
A half centimeter away
Bravo!
But you remain intertwined with striation
Assaulted at whim

Why do you continue
To skid along edges?
You flail about
Wallowing in indecision
Hoping to see the full moon
On a new moon afternoon
Wishing for the stars
Looking for grace, again

You have eyes

Do you not see?

Come closer

See?

I am the face of the moon

I liven the stars from within

Commit to me and see

I am always here

TRUELY SURRENDERED

Surrender happened this morning
As soon as there was
No answer
No response
No way out
There was realization

Then, Un-surrender happened
As soon as
Something desired
Even rather insignificant
Turned favorable
There was an about turn

Continuing a lifetime
Of dial and redial
It's the same number
The ringtone has not changed

But expectations
Change with every attempt
Every season
Each new season
Thought thinks
It can control the outcome

Total Irrevocable Surrender
Happens
Each moment
In the moment
When there's no need for retort
When non-reflection on original thought
Is instantaneous
And there's complete recognition
You know, not with the mind

When surrender truly happens
Stay attentive
Or you'll miss it

Performing Arts

You are an act

My activity

My operation

My display of dramatic flair

My great flamboyant performance

In my royal theatre

You, the extravagant show on stage

Albeit an interesting story

Is of no consequence

The Act is mine

Mine to create

Mine to commission

Mine to direct

You showcase

As an exhilarating performance

When you know and feel

In your heart and in your gut

When there is no doubt

That the you that you think you are

That image of you in your mind

Is worth not more than an image

That the idea of you in your head

Is precisely that! – an idea

It is not doing anything

It cannot do anything

It is being done.

PARTICLES & WAVES

Particles that bounce towards each other
They draw on one another
Amidst
Waves that do not subscribe to a prescribed pattern
Waves that do not adhere to rules
They flow a different direction
On a separate discourse

Your particles draw on mine
Mine are happy to welcome
Two amorous lovers
Dazzled by the other's movement
They converge west of sunset
They embrace
And emerge as one cluster at sunrise
Before they disperse

Midway east of sunrise
Our wavelength diverges
My waves falter and move north
Yours V lines and branches off
Southbound

Wavelengths in opposite directions
Equidistance
From their first point of encounter

Our particles still converge and embrace
Continued attraction that maintains
An after-hours schedule
Of collision without wavering
But our waves are on a course
Of permanent dissonance

Show & Tell

Show me your fears
I will lead you to its source

Tell me a secret
I will grant you restitution

Hand me your unease
I will purge indulgence

Show me your heart
I will tell you how it beats

Breathe for me
I will reveal myself to you

My Being is yours
No Charge!

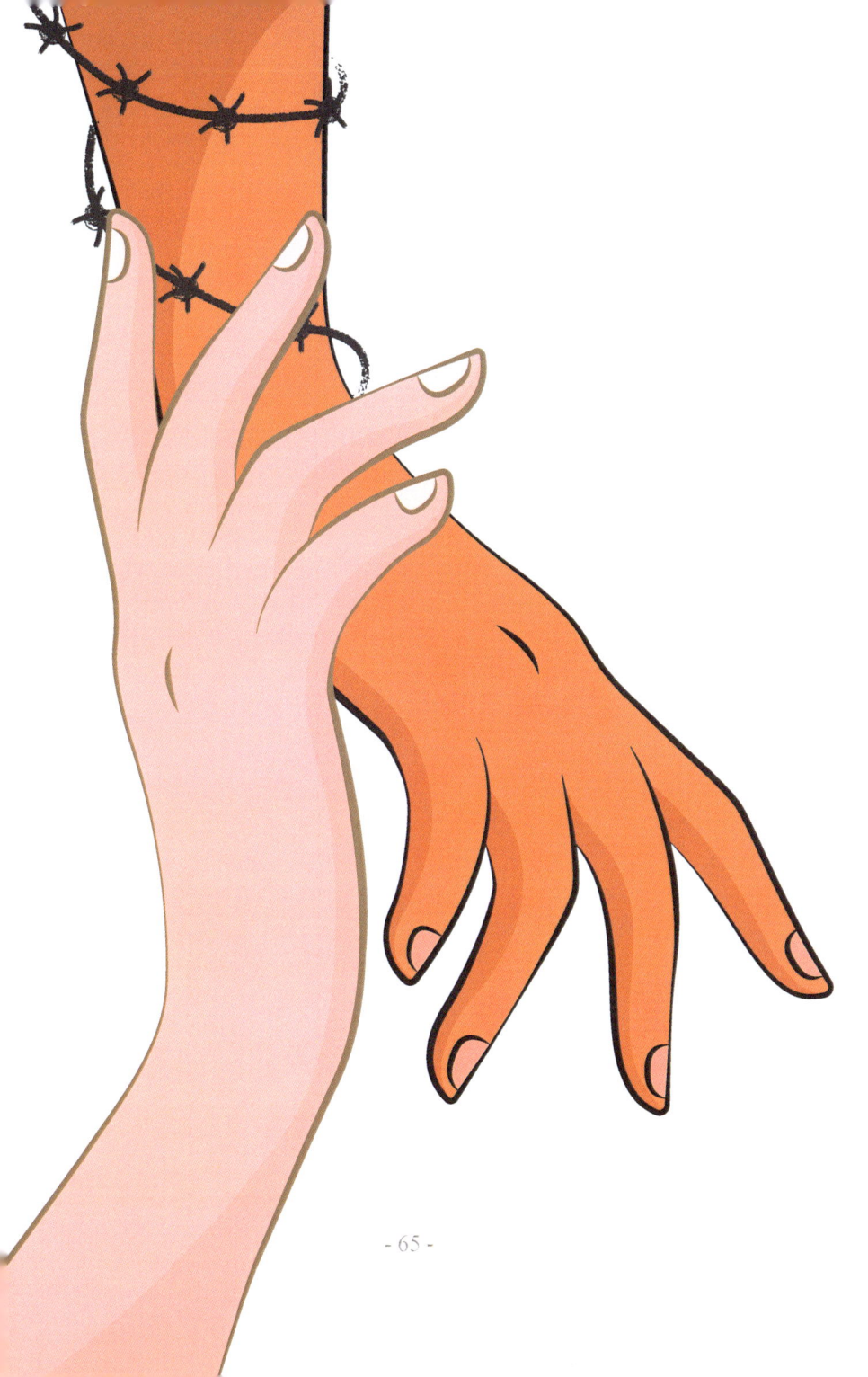

NOMENCLATURE

Do you feel better
Once you give me a name?
Now that you have a name for me
Do you know me any better?
When you call out my name
Can you hold me closer?

Does uttering my name
Alter your frame of reference?
Is your point of view
Now superior to a moment before?
Are your delusions about me
Any less fantastic?

Now that we both have earthly names
Different names
Are you entitled to finer things?
More possessions?

Why do you insist on foolishness?

Was I not already present

At my naming ceremony?

With or without a name

I am

DEVOTION

Do not lose grip
On devotion
Give me a name
And call my name
If it helps devotion

But
If romance with devotion
Conflicts with expectations
Is irreconcilable with veiled timetables
If unwavering devotion
Clashes with surreptitious agenda
Is discordant with deception
Incompatible with covert programs

If

Devotion fails

Be quiet

Stay silent

And remain still

Simply feel into me

Stay tuned to me

And stay awake

You must not fall back asleep!

WHERE WERE YOU?

When I appeared
Unannounced
To survey the realm

When I slid
To the foreground
To set the stage
For the next scene

Early mornings
Soon after a blink
Away fell my presence
For useless routine

CREATIVE IMPULSE

The farce in advertising
The farse marketing
My move to propagate
These are but features
Features of an impulse
My eternal impulse to create

It may appear exaggerated
Feel disconcerting at times, yes
But make not the mistake
Entangle not this impulse
Trace it back
Channel it; Claim it

Use it
For true undertakings
For profound experiences
Allow my bidding to unfold

A CROSSING

Late to bed
Early to rise
A lifetime of planning
In jeopardy

An appointed meeting
A monumental moment
At risk

I see your tired eyes
Wipe sleepiness away
We must meet
A planned crossing awaits

When you bump into me
It is not by accident
You must stay awake
Far more interesting things await

ALONENESS

A gift of time

A time for abidance

A blessing

Away from the sorority of comfort

Far from the brotherhood of emotional ease

The crowd of loneliness

Abide with me

Learn to love your time with me

Moments with me alone

Nurture my love

You are not alone

You are being held

Warmly in my arms

An Imagined Maze

Steeped deep

In high hedge

Zig zags of tall hedges

Intertwined

Feels like a maze

And in the thickness

There is panic

There must be ample dead ends!

But, choose consciously!

See?

There are only "right" turns

Whichever path you embark

Wherever you end up

I am there to greet you

With a sign

Clear and in large capital letters

WELCOME HOME!

Suspension

Do not fill my ears

With vain chatter

Listen to the reverberation of my unborn soul

Why tie up my heart

With useless worries

Why allow obligation to become a burden

And dwell on absolution

Untether the spigot

Swoosh

That is not a crash

Pivot

Suspend anticipation

Be carried from swirl to flow

Lose yourself

MISBEHAVIOR

Watch yourself misbehave
Ignore the heart
Indulge impulses
Redirect yearning
Contrary to wholeness
Push stability aside

Resign yourself from course correction
Misalign with growth
Internalize
Express your tyranny
Your rottenness
Lash out wantonly

Amuse yourself with misbehavior
Pull your earlobes for attention
A half smile
Conscious recognition
Of conditioned habit

INCLUSIVITY

Be deliberate

Choose singularity

Shift away from the overshadow

From active resistance

You have equitable access

Foster my sense of belonging

A sense of Being

Beyond tolerance

Embrace me

You belong to me

DEFLECTION

Behold, I remember
And continue to choose
To reflect this aspect of me
Appearing as you
A ceaseless ingress and egress

Do not be abashed
For behold, I also choose
To cease my deflection, momentarily
To know myself
To know you no longer as a name

THE PLAYER

A soccer ball
Resting at my feet
A basketball tucked under arm
A boxing glove fitted to hand
A racquet in a firm grip
Tight to swing
Tennis, Squash, Racquetball

I am on both sides
I am in all corners
The court, the ring, the field

The game you call life
I play
I play the "yes" and the "no"
To win and to lose
The intensity of my intension
All the same

Morning Glories

Do not close your heart
While I shine on you
Be like morning glories
When it salutes the sun
When it opens to greet the day
A show of flamboyant appreciation
Strutting trumpets of lilac and blue

Open Up
Expose Yourself
Let your naked bud bloom
Prepare to Launch
Unabashed and with delight

Cat & Mouse

Open the cupboards
Unhook the screens
The floorboards may need inspection too!
Keep the chase

Caught by the tail, almost
A near miss
Where's the mouse?
Who's the cat?
What's the game we play?
When does it end?
How does it end?

Try the other direction

To be certain, turn around

I am right behind you

I walk towards you, always

Let's meet soon

Bring this amusing delightful game

To an animated close

SIDEBAR

Ambush

Camouflaged as privacy

Never mind

Speak aloud

The union of space remains

Two Way Mirror

Space of the void
Steps to the unknown
Reflecting
Shallow or deep down
Forward or backward
Outward or Inward
The medium appears fixed

At Ease
It's a fluke
An imaginary boundary
Outwardly, desire for something
Inwardly, fear of something
Pull a key piece out from the block
Notice the grumble
Watch the foundation crumble

Leave the desire be

Befriend the fear as is

Better yet

Pop the bubble

The harsh pop happens

Only in the moment

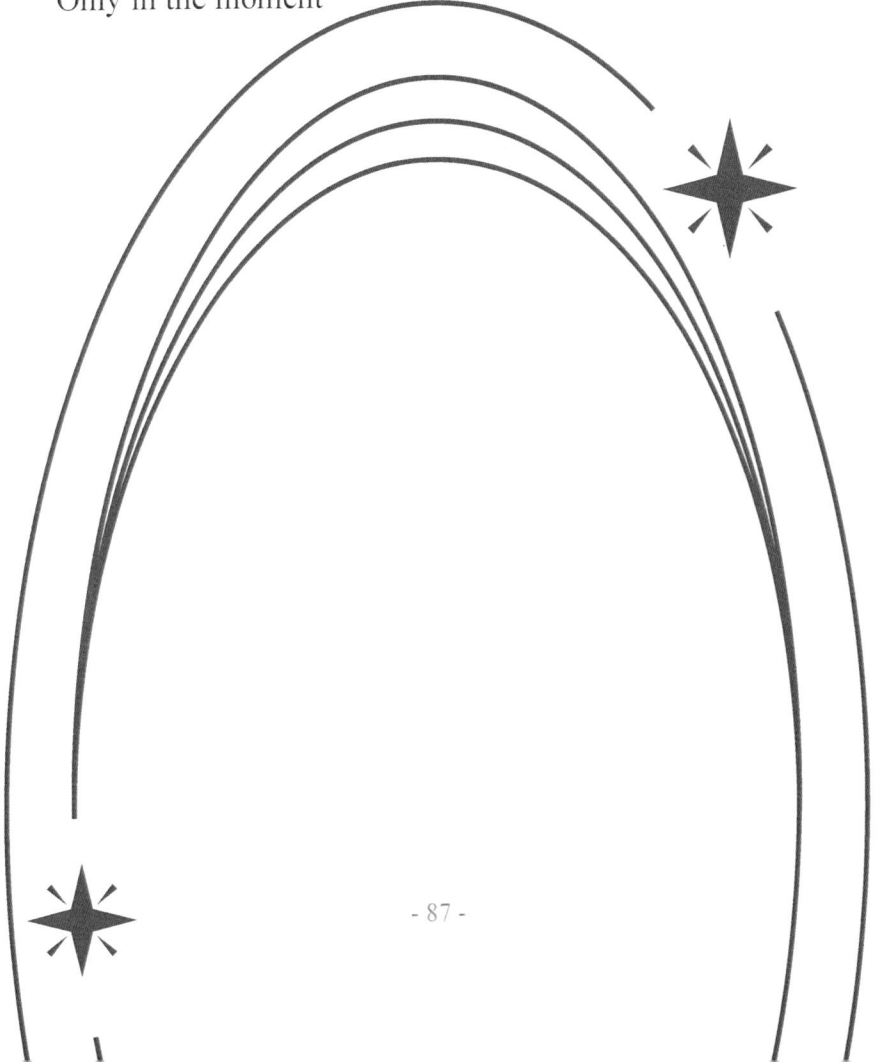

The Peacock and The Swan

Strutting plumes

Designs and colors

Of effortless beauty and grace

A reflection of free flowing kriya

Of spiritual balance

Invoking natural appreciation

An unimpeded flow of gratitude

CREATING CREATION

Creation

Unplugged

Surrendered to divine flow

Generating equations without formulas

Unnumbered inceptions from birth

Of bespoke gadgets

Unending live streams

The Creator

Creating through creation

I & I

Open your arms

For a bigger embrace

Open your arms wide

Let me in unrestrained

Let me indulge in familiarity

In light unfiltered

For in union

I and I are one

DISBELIEF

Dear believer
Devoid of faith
Shall I repeat?

There is Nothing
On either side of the moon
Nothing more deserving of attention
Than what is
Deep in your heart
You know this to be true

You beckon for Nothing
Yet shut the door
As soon as it arrives at your doorstep
Rather than welcome in Nothing
You insist on negotiations
Useless efforting
Negotiating a timely demise

What use is belief?

Or disbelief?

Waiting?

Dreaming up an exit strategy?

Manna will surely descend?

Must you believe

What you already know?

Do you not know

What you know?

Do you know

What you don't know?

You of limited duration

Your time got over

Le Stage est fini

That shack is burning

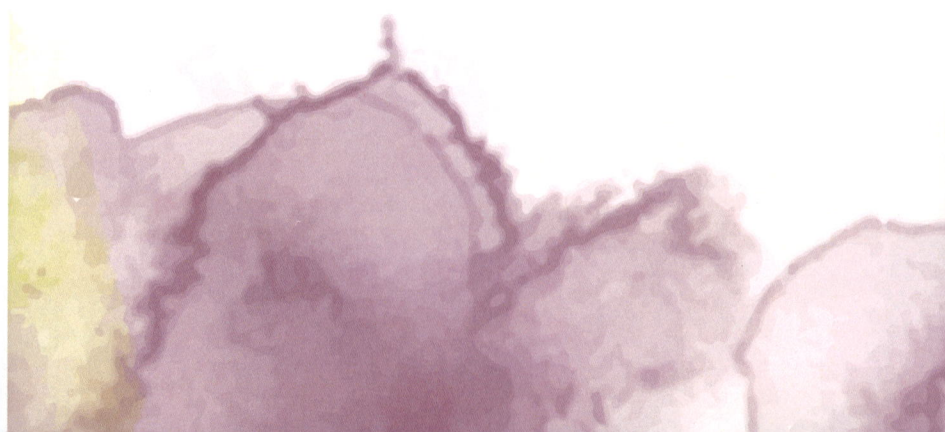

Leave now

Run to me

Through the fire

I shall hose you clean

Of residual soot

Relieve you of untimely existence

An imminent disappearance

Port you to my table

Manna is plentiful

BOTTEGA

Tossing and turning

Do you dislike the scenery to the left?

You look up

Were you not aware of the blueness of the sky?

You turn away from it, facedown

Something has not gone your way?

You are no longer in slumber

Why not wake up completely?

Yawn asleepness away

Stretch out your dulled arms

Stand up from fixed positionality

Look around

Whichever way you turn

See that it is merely a different view

A different view of the same room

It is the same space

My Bottega

Turn and toss as you desire

She does not object

SCORPION LEAF

Tiny leaflets

Dancing in the wind

Stalls of scorpion imagery

Crawling midair

Pushing against space

An open display

At the intersection

Of earth and wind

With the center of space

As background

QUICKSILVER

Circles with no lines

Squares without angles

Pointless Places

The restriction of oppositions

The vastness of conjunctions

Symbols and Omens

Dreams

Mysticism and Paradoxes

Faces without names

Bodies with no contours

Lovers of a kind

Without boundaries

SADHGURU
(A DEDICATION)

My little one
How did everyday noise
Puny affairs
Pitiable, trifling stories
Become a grand affair?

Consistent howling
Colossal display of trivial incidents
How did the negligible
Become aggrandized clamor?
Much ado about so little
A tribute to ignorance

I can see
Ner' ending movement
Paddling, very hard
But infinitely in circles
Endless unsustainable efforting

Come to me

When fatigued

Reach for me

There is something else

Ecstasy of nothingness

TEARS OF CHIOS

A banquet is prepared
A feast awaits
Renowned guests in attendance

At the head of the table
A distinguished guest sits
Lost in mental activity
Nibbling at side dishes
Shifting edibles
To corners of the platter
Uninterested in the main dish

Here is what's on offer
An open invitation
A long-standing invitation
A mystical mastic
Not unlike Tears of Chios

Chew quietly, intently
Taste the flavor
Bitter on first bite?

Savor it slowly
The bitterness dissipates
Releasing bountiful goodness
On afterbite
Without an aftertaste
Until at the end
Nothing is revealed

Marvel at nothingness
Revel in ecstasy

IMAGE

The texture of hair

The prominence of forehead

The shape of eyebrows

Grooves around the nose

Contours of ears

Dimples gracing cheeks

Liquid lips of pure sound

A structured chin

Determined to serve as foundation

Your face

An emblem of my image

AURORAL MIST

An existence of contractions
A lifetime of contradictions
Advances in incongruity
A course of paradox

Analogs of dichotomy
Like the rebounding streak of Bamboo
And the ethereal hues of Auroral Mist

Simple organic elements
Unfolding abstract curtains
Distinct shapeless whispers
Of inspired creation

FAITH

Smile

As the Sunflower to the sun

An open salute, unfailingly

Bow

As the Whispering Bell to fire

A graceful acknowledgement of credence, unpretentiously

Embrace

As the Trailing Rosemary to a wall

In complete, total reliance, elegantly

Trust

As the English Ivy

Resilient, Tolerant, Fidel, Eternally

IMPERSONATION

On Stage
Live the dream fully
Enjoy yourself
It's part of the play

A las, come backstage
Take off the costume
Bit by bit, if necessary
I'll help with the undress

Begin with shoes
They weigh a ton
Heavy on the landing
The oversized, scuffed jacket too!
Your disappearance act with it
Was most convincing
Now, peel off the mask
Layered tightly to the skin

A las, face the mirror
Ready for the reveal
Look, it is my face
Your true image

Take a good look
Sketch not only the profile
Etch every bit of the silhouette
Draw bold lines over the outliers
Immerse your attention completely
Absorb my full essence

A las, it is curtain call
Hop back on stage
Acknowledge the applause
Without forgetting
No memory lapse
Remember your real image
Do not ignore your true self

THE SURVEYOR

Appreciate the landscape
Filled with grooves and rough ridges
An eternity of marked time
Littered emotions abandoned on earth

Don't lose footing
Processions of storms continue
Swirling with intent
Forging undeterred
Crashing one by one
Uneasy holds a tight grudge

Another one soon comes
Roaring
Let me in!
Before I crash again
Let me go!
There are clear skies in my wake

DROP THE ACT, ALREADY!

Talking head

Bundle of memory

Medium of imagination

The likes and dislikes

The tantric violence

The tyranny of the tyrant

All are plays

On divine stage

But, you are swelled up with angst

Engorged by ignorance

Who are you to suppress or express?

The tyrant is mere activity

Tyranny is movement of activity

You are not

I am

And, I am passing through

Fully embodied

Informed Moving Attention

Infused with Pure Intelligence

THE MEETING PLACE

Desire and fullness
Meet at fulfillment
Where what you want
Is what you have
Where every contra desire
Non-wants and non-likes
Are also available

It's all here
Choose what you don't like
Or drop it for a better non-desire

Likes, dislikes
Wishes
Desires, non-desires
These are all survivors of Epoch
At the Meeting Place

Soulmates On The Run

Fastidiously tracking your level of consciousness

When you finally reach a last stance

You find forgetfulness

A friendly nemesis

Smiling, beckoning

It invites you to rest

Your weary bones need respite

Forgetfulness and comfort

A couple not unlike

Same kind companions

Soulmates on the run

Don't get lazy

Comfort paired with forgetfulness

Alienates vibrancy from consciousness

Forgetfulness in comfort

Forgoes the face of consciousness

Eternity never lost

And never found

BURNING CURRENT

Ashes

Residues of burning expressions

Of vexation and distaste

Diabolical thoughts

Caught in cycles

Preoccupied with tracking?

Merits and demerits?

But outpaced by the Current?

Glitchy moments?

Delayed recognition?

Always a step late?

Worry not

The fire still burns, fervently

The light of the fire is Current

And the Current pervades

Sooner or later

Spirit with intense zeal

Transmutes irritation, loathing

The dullest

The most forgetful

Even the most lethargic

Your Favorite Things

How can I compete
With your most precious thing
For as long as it is around
You are inattentive
When it is lost
When you tire of it
When it dies
You'll come to me

I shall wait
Do not kneel in supplication
Afterall, your precious things
Are gifts of myself
The very act of their dissipation
Is a revelation
A renewal and a revival
Of the giver

CONVOCATION

Evocation
Flowing gowns of color
Bright faces smiling
Caps flown high to the wind
Moments of celebration follow

But you have returned
Searching...
A pile of debris to sort through

What are you searching for?
Your symbol of pride?
A lost memory?

Convocation is also initiation
A transient experience, yes
But timeless, groundless invocation
So, hold the tassel loose
And stay Awake!

Dark Snow

Stained by dirt
Mixed with earth
The cookie crumbles
Not in vain

Foresight
Shadow blindness
Hindsight
Now is not barren

BLURB

You are distraught
Over slight movement
A small disturbance
A minor inconvenience
An insignificant hassle
And you are compelled
To invent and formulate a story
Old matter
Rehashed, rehearsed and presented
As new, unique content

You have bought into the promotions, understandably
But remember
You are no more than a Blurb
Filled with ordinary content
Inconsequential descriptives and summaries
A cover appearance
On a blank page

Tapioca

An acquired taste
Of clouded and murky waters
Wholesome and guaranteed crisp
With a good rinse

A mystifying fascination
Of body's karmic impurities
Impeccably functional
Purified with conscious breath

MOCKERY

Breath of my soul

Infused

With a bit of character

Smirking

Puppet on a string

Highlights for my carnival

Freedom Undefined

Soak

Float

Drift in unboundedness

When rubble and friction

Push hard

Remain unperturbed at water's edge

Waves of myself

Orchestrate a breathing space

And carry with ease

Bask

In freedom undefined

THE RETURN

Coming home is an arduous undertaking
Flags in the air
Signs on earth
Posts in space
Markings on land
All navigation tools
To guide that semicircular trip back
A concaved journey home

You would think
Abandon a simple task
It's an easy road that lies ahead
Afterall, the pocketbook is empty
And the low trunk is useless
Crammed with worthless resources
Exhausted nonfunctional tools

Forget not the upper trunk
It too is defunct
Filled with futile ideas
Pointless, aimless strategies
Non workable plans, really

But abandon powered by surrender
Tis motivation not enough!
And for the prodigal
There are no guarantees
Of a convergent return
Of settling back, Embodied
Creation, intricately woven
Presents limitless opportunities
To be distracted; to be caught
The playground
Once replete with subtle, hidden distractions
The kind that led and kept away
Still has an abundance of the same kind
Now appearing blatantly in plain sight
Beckoning; Still enticing
But harsh, with a bitter aftertaste

Entangling, flagrant and heavy
Daring a step toward home
A thousand more steps away

But, one is deplete
Of resources
Of decisive ideas
Of divisive imaginations
Of a "purported" will power

Alas, there's Yoga!
One must stumble less
Make fewer pit stops
And focus attention
Directly on The Return

The Return to life at home
Is a return to conscious wisdom
Still; Dynamic
With drops of liquid Ambrosia
Dripping and flowing through the core
And an expansive vista
Preview of a Return
To life living itself

www.ingramcontent.com/pod-product-compliance
Lightning Source LLC
Chambersburg PA
CBRC090845120626
46551CB00011B/760